You are special, and Brad Friedman wants to make sure you know it. Get periodic insights from Brad by subscribing to his special email list. Just send an email to brad@friedmansocialmedia.com and write in the subject line, "THiNKaha book." He'll take it from there.

Brad Friedman on Digital Marketing

Doing Social Media Right, When You Don't Have the Time and Don't Want to Get in Trouble

Brad Friedman

An Actionable Business Journal

E-mail: info@thinkaha.com
20660 Stevens Creek Blvd., Suite 210
Cupertino, CA 95014

⇨ Please go to http://aha.pub/DigitalMarketing to read this AHAbook and to share the individual AHAmessages that resonate with you.

Published by THiNKaha®
20660 Stevens Creek Blvd., Suite 210, Cupertino, CA 95014
http://thinkaha.com
E-mail: info@thinkaha.com

First Printing: October 2017
Hardcover ISBN: 978-1-61699-227-9   1-61699-227-1
Paperback ISBN: 978-1-61699-228-6   1-61699-228-X
eBook ISBN: 978-1-61699-226-2   1-61699-226-3
Place of Publication: Silicon Valley, California, USA
Paperback Library of Congress Number: 2017952454

Trademarks

All terms mentioned in this book that are known to be trademarks or service marks have been appropriately capitalized. Neither THiNKaha, nor any of its imprints, can attest to the accuracy of this information. Use of a term in this book should not be regarded as affecting the validity of any trademark or service mark.

Warning and Disclaimer

Every effort has been made to make this book as complete and as accurate as possible. The information provided is on an "as is" basis. The author(s), publisher, and their agents assume no responsibility for errors or omissions. Nor do they assume liability or responsibility to any person or entity with respect to any loss or damages arising from the use of information contained herein.

Dedication

This book is dedicated to small business owners and professional services providers everywhere, especially those who want to have a professional online presence and those who understand they must have an online presence to compete, but need to do it in a way that complies with the rules and regulations they are bound by.

I'd also like to acknowledge my father, Sheldon Friedman, whose first of three books was published when he was eighty-two years old. He's my hero and my inspiration.

Finally, this book is also dedicated to my wife and children: Laurie, Brandon, and Lauren. There aren't enough words in the English language to describe how much I love you. You inspire me every day by just being you and doing what you do. Thank you for your love and support.

How to Read a THiNKaha® Book
A Note from the Publisher

The THiNKaha series is the CliffsNotes of the 21st century. The value of these books is that they are contextual in nature. Although the actual words won't change, their meaning will change every time you read one as your context will change. Experience your own "AHA!" moments ("AHAmessages™") with a THiNKaha book; AHAmessages are looked at as "actionable" moments—think of a specific project you're working on, an event, a sales deal, a personal issue, etc. and see how the AHAmessages in this book can inspire your own AHAmessages, something that you can specifically act on. Here's how to read one of these books and have it work for you:

1. Read a THiNKaha book (these slim and handy books should only take about 15–20 minutes of your time!) and write down one to three actionable items you thought of while reading it. Each journal-style THiNKaha book is equipped with space for you to write down your notes and thoughts underneath each AHAmessage.

2. Mark your calendar to re-read this book again in 30 days.

3. Repeat step #1 and write down one to three more AHAmessages that grab you this time. I guarantee that they will be different than the first time. BTW: this is also a great time to reflect on the actions taken from the last set of AHAmessages you wrote down.

After reading a THiNKaha book, writing down your AHAmessages, re-reading it, and writing down more AHAmessages, you'll begin to see how these books contextually apply to you. THiNKaha books advocate for continuous, lifelong learning. They will help you transform your ahas into actionable items with tangible results until you no longer have to say "AHA!" to these moments—they'll become part of your daily practice as you continue to grow and learn.

As The AHA Guy at THiNKaha, I definitely practice what I preach. I read 2-3 AHAbooks a month in addition to those that we publish and take away two to three different action items from each of them every time. Please e-mail me your AHAs today!

Mitchell Levy
publisher@thinkaha.com

Contents

Foreword

We are living in an ever-changing world. The way people communicate today is much different than it was when I graduated from Tufts University and went to work as an analyst at Lehman Brothers in the late 1980s. After a few years with Lehman Brothers, the entrepreneurial bug took over, and I founded, ran, and sold three independent businesses. Over the years, I've seen the way people communicate change.

Today, people do nearly everything online. It's how we buy things. It's how we research the things we buy and the people or businesses we buy things from. We decide where we're going to eat online. We choose dentists, doctors, accountants, and lawyers online. We start with Google, Bing, Yahoo, or another search engine. We ask our online friends, family, colleagues, and even strangers to give us buying advice.

This shift to the internet has also forever changed the world of marketing. Back in the day, marketers focused on television and radio ads, billboards, direct mail, seminars, and more. Today, businesses of all sizes have shifted large portions of their marketing dollars to digital marketing.

Digital marketing has leveled the playing field. Companies large and small must play by the same rules online. Large companies may have more money and larger marketing staffs, but they still must play by the same rules. Having a great presence on the internet is essential. Sharing value-add content is also necessary. Your leads and prospects are researching your product or service right now. All you have to do is be there when they click. You've got to be found when they come searching for you.

This new world of marketing comes with new rules. Along with those new rules, business owners must shift their thinking from old-world marketing techniques to today's digital marketing tactics. Putting aside something you're familiar with can be challenging. It's human nature to continue to do the things we're comfortable with.

Lucky for us, we've got Brad Friedman to be our guide in this new marketing world. I've worked with Brad myself, and he's worked with hundreds of other businesses of all different sizes. His background as an attorney allows him to look at things a little differently. His experience and knowledge of digital marketing strategies and tactics can match up against anyone. It's just our luck he's gathered the many years of his experience and shared it with us.

In this book, you'll find digital marketing strategy and tactics from Brad and others. You'll find practical advice and ideas you can implement in your business today. You'll see anyone can do this and do this ... well, right now.

Don't wait another minute to dive in and start reading. Enter with an open mind and a willingness to try new things to succeed in the business world we live in today.

Jeffrey Shavitz
#1 Amazon Bestselling Author of *Size Doesn't Matter—*
Why Small Business Is BIG Business
Chief Golf Officer at
http://www.clickitgolf.com/
Twitter.com/JeffShavitz
www.jeffshavitz.com

Introduction

Building a professional online presence is a challenge—especially if you must do this and comply with regulations. Many business owners know they have to have an online presence to compete, but they think digital marketing is silly. I often hear, "Social media? That's not something businesses do. That's what my kids spend most of their day doing." Right! It's also something consumers of products and services spend portions of their days doing. And social media is only one tool we must learn to utilize in our digital marketing toolbox.

Quick example: I'll bet before you buy a product online or in person, you "google it," research it, and read the reviews your peers have left. The same is true if you're looking for a new dentist, doctor, CPA, lawyer, or financial services provider. It's the way we operate in the world today.

This book will help you understand the challenges of using digital marketing in a professional manner, one that's in compliance with the regulations that govern your industry. Creating and implementing a winning digital marketing strategy can be a tough chore for any type of business, but it is arguably the most challenging for those firms engaged in the world of professional services. Here are six challenges to think about as you read the book:

1. "Blah" Subject Matter. Let's face it: reading about asset allocations, tax efficiency, or diversification is, for most people, not terribly exciting. But while not exciting, this information is still important. Therein lies the challenge from a digital marketing standpoint: how do you create excitement and buzz about topics that don't lend themselves well to flashy marketing? Dynamic, compliant content is possible with the right mix of creative marketing and industry know-how.

2. Complexity. A medical diagnosis, legal opinion, or recitation of this year's revisions to the tax code can be complicated subjects, both for the end-consumer and for the digital marketer tasked with creating marketing content. In an effort to write at a level consumers will understand, professional services marketers will sometimes try to "dumb down" the message. However, doing so can create huge headaches from a regulatory standpoint, and it's also doing the reader a disservice. The challenge is to interpret and describe difficult concepts in a way readers will "get," while engaging them to want to learn more. To be honest, the same is true for the owner of your favorite Pilates studio or sandwich shop.

3. Consumer Trust. After the scandals of the last decades, including the highly publicized Ponzi scheme perpetrated by Bernie Madoff, investors are skittish when it comes to financial services firms—for good reason. Any perception that a firm or its salespeople are too "salesy" can send a potential client running in the other direction. The tone of digital marketing communications needs to strike the right balance between knowledge and experience, and salesmanship. But this isn't a reason to stay away from the internet. It's a reason to be careful and thoughtful about what you do on there, so you are able to maintain your license.

4. Embracing the Digital Age. Financial services firms have been slower than other industries to adapt to using social media to communicate with clients, but having a social media presence (and using it effectively) is critical in today's digital environment. According to various data, there is evidence that spending on digital marketing is increasing for professional services firms and businesses of all sizes. As a matter of fact, there are many reports that business owners are shifting funds from traditional marketing avenues to digital marketing.

5. Reaching the Next Generation of Consumers. A financial firm may have been working with different generations of a family for decades, but if their digital marketing communications don't "speak to" the next generation, they may not be able to retain the business over the long term. Marketing messages that appeal to one generation may not appeal to, or may even alienate, another generation.

The key is striking the right balance so marketing messages appeal to clients at any stage of life. Finding the right words to use online is important to restaurant owners, retail shop owners, and others. We've heard a lot of talk about Millennials, Gen Xers, and other labels we've put on various generations. Presenting your professional persona properly is critical to staying in business over the long haul.

6. Regulatory Considerations and Restrictions. Regulatory concerns are probably the biggest challenge facing professional services firms today. Professional services firms are subject to a laundry list of regulations, depending on the types of products and services the firm offers. They may be subject to rules promulgated by the SEC, FINRA, state insurance departments, and/or the Department of Labor. They may be subject to the Code of Professional Responsibility, HIPAA, AICPA Standards and Regulations, and more. And there are numerous city and state rules and regulations governing every other type of business you can think of. The myriad rules (and their interpretations) can be complex and confusing, and violations can have far-reaching consequences. Taking care to mold a professional online persona is worth the work, the time, and the money.

Business owners and professionals' digital marketing materials can build and keep consumer's trust and loyalty and can utilize social media channels and more to attract the next generation of clients without being overly conservative, boring, or complicated. All of this is possible while still being in full compliance with regulatory requirements, but it is critical that digital marketers have their finger on the pulse of the industry, fully understand the rules and regulations that apply, and understand how to operate within that framework to create dynamic, effective content.

Sit back, relax, and enjoy the rest of this book. It's filled with the wisdom and experience of many different people.

Section I
Digital Marketing Strategy

If you don't know where you're going or how you're going to get there, how do you know when you've arrived? Having a digital marketing strategy is essential to your success!

It's important you take the time to identify your target audience and hone your message to them. You've got to research where your audience hangs out online and develop your presence there. Are people looking for wealth managers on Instagram or LinkedIn? We all have only so much bandwidth to market with. Making strategic decisions about who your target audience is, where they hang out, and what message will resonate with them is critical to your success.

Can you do this on your own? Do you have someone on your staff who's able to do this kind of work? If the answer is "No," then contract for the work that needs to get done. Business owners often hesitate to look outside their team for resources. My feeling is you got where you are by focusing on your core competencies. And if developing and implementing a digital marketing strategy is not one of your core competencies, contract with someone to do this essential work for you.

Need a Digital Marketing Consultant? Three Important Questions to Ask

Do you need a digital marketing consultant? A major component of a small business's online success lies in their ability to implement an effective digital marketing strategy. The digital marketing world is always moving, changing, and growing

With that said, digital marketing can be an intimidating topic to tackle, let alone building a strategy from scratch. It's no wonder a small business marketing budget survey revealed nearly half of small businesses allocate 20 percent or less of their marketing budget to digital marketing.

It's incredibly difficult to uncover an online marketing channel that works consistently! It takes time, testing, and know-how, each of which most small business owners are not the least bit interested in, especially when they're focused on the big-picture aspects of running a business.

A digital marketing consultant or agency creates strategic online marketing plans tailored to help your brand gain recognition. While the primary goal of a digital marketing consultant is to increase the sales numbers of a company's products or services, the real benefit in using a consultant lies in their ability to generate online brand awareness.

The potential to spread your brand's message throughout the internet like wildfire is a powerful thing. A digital marketing consultant's plan for a business may include a series of guerrilla marketing tactics that help realize the underlying goal.

Aside from giving your business actionable ideas and opinions from an objective perspective, there are plenty of benefits for small to medium-sized businesses using a digital marketing consultant.

Save Marketing Team Costs

While some digital marketing consultants come with a seemingly heavy price tag, consultants are much more affordable compared to hiring your own in-house professional digital marketing team. As a rough example of what a digital marketing team would cost, here's the average salary for some professionals in the digital marketing field.

- Digital Marketing Manager - $73,000

- Social Media Manager - $49,000

- SEO Marketing Expert - $60,000

- Web Designer - $47,000

- Graphic Designer - $53,000

- Copywriter - $55,000

So, if you went out and hired a team of experienced freelance professionals like the group above, you'd be looking at a pretty steep bill running into the tens of thousands of dollars a month. And that doesn't include the benefits package you would provide.

A digital marketing consultant or agency would likely cost much less and provide the same marketing value—with a twist.

Scaled Marketing Efforts

Through the traditional in-house marketing hiring method, the only way you would be able to increase your marketing output to see better results would be to hire more employees.

Consultancy agencies have access to teams of skilled individuals able to implement changes in a digital marketing strategy at a moment's notice.

Keeping Up with Digital Marketing Trends

A team of in-house marketers usually doesn't have much time to read up on the latest graphic design, SEO, or social media marketing trends. And they don't have time to tell you all about them.

With a digital marketing consultant, however, you gain access to the latest internet marketing trends from an educated individual whose job is knowing what changes might be lurking around the corner. This means staying up to date with the latest Google algorithm changes and knowing which marketing channels are best suited to your business's niche.

Now that you know a few of the major benefits that come with hiring a digital marketing consultant, let's talk about three key questions to ask potential consultants or agencies.

1. What Have You Done in the Past?

You need to get a rough idea of what your prospective consultant has done for customers in the past, both online and off. It's great to find a digital marketing consultant who offers a list of previous clients and includes their testimonials.

If you want to be really thorough, contact a few former clients and ask about their experiences. This way, you get a good idea of how the consultant communicates, as well as their areas of expertise. It's also wise to favor candidates who've worked in your industry or a similar industry before.

2. What Can You Do for Me Now?

After you've obtained an outline of a consultant's track record, you need to find out exactly what it is they can do for your business. Does their skill set complement your business niche? Have they published any articles in major magazines or authoritative websites? What can the consultant offer that their competitors cannot?

3. What about Our Current Marketing Plan?

It's vital to have a prospective consultant give you their honest input on your current digital marketing plan. When giving them your plan, it's also important to provide them with context on your current situation.

If they supply you with a semi-automated reply that gives you no indication they paid attention to your current unique situation, then you might be better off seeking a consultant who's willing to pay attention to the small details. On the flip side, if you received a detailed response outlining an honest assessment of your marketing efforts, including your plan's strengths and weaknesses, then you may have a winner.

There are an endless number of ways you can gauge the efficacy of a digital marketing consultant. Knowing what you want in a consultant, as well as what to ask, are the first steps toward realizing a more effective digital marketing strategy for your small business.

1

Zig Zigler said, "You were born to win, but to be a winner, you must plan to win, prepare to win, and expect to win." @BradFriedman

_____

_____

_____

2

On the other end is a human being with all the hopes, dreams, and fears you yourself have. Your message MUST tap into this. @BradFriedman

_____

_____

_____

3

Every business doesn't need a presence on every social channel. Be strategic. Go where your prospects hang out. @BradFriedman

_____

_____

_____

4

If you're not measuring, you're not marketing. @BradFriedman

_____

_____

_____

5

I firmly believe people do business with people, not businesses. Use your social presence to develop relationships. @BradFriedman

_____

_____

_____

6

In the real world, we want to do business with people we trust. Social Media is the real world. Use it to develop trust. @BradFriedman

_____

_____

_____

7

We want to do business with people we find credible. Social Media is the real world. Use it to develop credibility. @BradFriedman

_____

_____

_____

8

Business owners don't have a choice about doing social media. But if your heart isn't really in it, you won't do it well.
@BradFriedman

_____

_____

_____

9

For the 1st time in history, we have tech that allows businesses to develop real relationships with huge numbers of people.
@BradFriedman

10

Digital Marketing levels the playing field and gives the small business owner an opportunity to compete with big brands.
@BradFriedman

11

People do biz with people, not businesses. Use your brand's social channels to develop relationships, trust, and credibility. @BradFriedman

_____

_____

_____

12

To survive, today's social CEO must know how to attract, engage, and grow their network on relevant social channels. @BradFriedman

_____

_____

_____

13

Spend an hour a day, every day, for 45 days, building your network, and the rewards will make you a true believer. @BradFriedman

_____

_____

_____

14

Make a commitment to social selling by opening up your personal self and your business self. Even if it's just a little. @BradFriedman

_____

_____

_____

15

Your digital marketing strategy must build awareness of you and your brand if you want to generate revenue. @BradFriedman

_____

_____

_____

16

Does your digital marketing strategy emphasize the word "COMMUNITY"? @BradFriedman

_____

_____

_____

17

Never forget: BEFORE we meet for you to give me your pitch, I know everything I need to know about you. @BradFriedman

_____

_____

_____

18

Every sale today of products and services, B2B & B2C, is preceded, even precluded, by your online presence. @BradFriedman

---

19

Are you still waiting for your lawyers to approve your digital marketing plan? WAKE UP and look at your competition! @BradFriedman

---

20

Smart executives span the competitive landscape to review the competition's digital presence on a regular basis. @BradFriedman

_____

_____

_____

21

Do your due diligence before contracting out your social media. Many can help and many more claim they can help.
@BradFriedman

_____

_____

_____

22

Millions of businesses display their social media logos on their websites. Do you? Get in the game! @BradFriedman

_____

_____

_____

23

The more value you offer, the more attractive your social community. More attractive = more prospects = more revenue. @BradFriedman

_____

_____

_____

24

Some keys to digital marketing success: act business-like, be proactive, and continually push out value-add content.
@BradFriedman

_____

_____

_____

25

Once you understand who already buys your product, you will know what corner of the market you've already covered.
@BradFriedman

_____

_____

_____

26

When you make problems look real and demonstrate how you solve them, it gives consumers a real view of the products you offer. @BradFriedman

_____

_____

_____

27

Publish new content to your blog often.
Make it relevant and interesting. Give your
visitors something of value to take away.
@BradFriedman

Section II
Facebook

I Bet You Didn't Know You Can Grow Your Email List with Facebook

With close to two billion monthly active users, Facebook is perhaps the best social platform to execute your social media marketing goals. Do some research and determine if your target audience actively uses Facebook first. Whether you desire to connect with customers, share your expertise, improve engagement, gain new leads, or close sales, Facebook marketing can help you meet your business' goals and build a strong presence online.

Since generating leads is the lifeline to your business, the objective here is to share a few creative ways on how you can successfully leverage Facebook to grow your email list. The key, however, is being crystal clear on your target audience (by developing buyer personas), knowing their pain points, and being the solution provider, so you're seen as a credible resource in your industry. Once this is established, the following tactics will be easier to implement.

#1. Go on the Air with Facebook Live!

Looking for a way to quickly capture the attention of your Facebook followers and stand out in their news feed? Latest figures show that people spend three times longer watching live video compared to pre-recorded video. Adding live-streaming video to your marketing mix improves engagement with your viewers, increases brand awareness, expands influence, and is another strategy to build your email list.

With Facebook Live, you can zero in on topics that resonate with your target audience, then extend exclusive promotions to gain new leads. Broadcasting ideas include delving deeper into popular blog posts, hosting a Q&A session, or taking viewers backstage at a live event.

#2. Design Landing Pages Exclusively for Your Facebook Followers

Having landing pages designated for your Facebook followers will greatly increase conversions because it is targeted, relates specifically to a content offer or message you've promoted on Facebook, and appeals to this exact audience.

Consider these pointers toward designing a winning landing page for your Facebook marketing:

- The landing page headline and advertising wording (whether from your Facebook ad or a post) should complement each other.

- Use images and videos that relate to the content to boost SEO and website experience.

- Ensure the CTA is strong and gives clear direction on what to do next.

- Make them super actionable, with content that goes deep into solving a problem.

- Long-form content of 1500-plus words also may improve SEO.

- Target keyword phrases your audience is actively searching for.

- Sell and demonstrate the benefits they'll receive in return for opting into your list.

Keep in mind: after you build your first landing page, you must continually test variations to improve your conversion metrics.

#3. Easily Follow Your Site Visitors Everywhere with Facebook Retargeting

Retargeting, or remarketing, is a paid strategy where you place a tracking code on your website that will set a tracking snippet, or cookie, on the browser of those who actually visit your website. This allows your ad content to "follow" your recent visitors wherever they go online. It's highly effective in keeping your brand top of mind after people click your ad or leave your website.

Facebook retargeting is extremely cost efficient and simple to implement. You're able to create custom audiences and tailor content specific to them for better responsiveness. This tactic should be one that is constantly running to maximize traffic and attract fresh, ongoing leads to your sales funnel.

#4. Give a Special Touch by Personally Reaching Out

Not a popular method yet extremely effective and valuable in building relationships with followers, personally contacting potential customers adds a special touch to your strategy and separates your company from competitors. You're expressing real interest in your prospects, and it shows you value their engagement with your brand. I firmly believe people do business with people, not businesses. It's all about taking the time to develop relationships.

You can simply ask a question that initiates conversation with your followers. Get their insight of your posts/content, your new product, or the services you offer. Requesting information like what their major pain points are is a great strategy to offer them your (free) content as a solution. Discover what their needs are, and share a link that leads to a landing page that gives the content offer.

Commit to choosing one to two of these strategies to begin converting Facebook followers into leads. With consistency, you'll experience growth in email subscribers and have more leads to nurture.

28

Facebook is like jail. You sit all day wasting time, talking to a wall & scrutinizing those who want to be friends with you.
@BradFriedman

_____

_____

_____

29

Before you click "post," remember the words you choose may be forgiven but never forgotten. You can't take 'em back! @BradFriedman

_____

_____

_____

30

Success on Facebook is about building a community of brand advocates who Like, Share, and Comment on your value-add content. @BradFriedman

_____

_____

_____

31

Businesses, remember Facebook is a social network, not a diary. Everything you post is public. @BradFriedman

_____

_____

_____

32

Facebook Addiction: Signing out of
Facebook on your computer only to get into
your car and log back in on your phone?
@BradFriedman

_____

_____

_____

33

Facebook says we are "Friends." Trust me,
I'll slap you upside the head if you post that
crap on my wall again. @BradFriedman

_____

_____

_____

34

I'm a firm believer that not every brand needs a Facebook page. Do some research. Go where your audience hangs out.
@BradFriedman

_____

_____

_____

Section III
Inbound Marketing

How Honesty Can Give an Edge to Your Inbound Marketing Strategy

Although inbound marketing has become very popular, many people still have doubts about whether it actually works. This is because inbound goes against much of what we've learned about marketing. When we think about marketing, we visualize a process of reaching out to the customer to convince them the product or service we're selling is worth the investment—i.e. we visualize outbound marketing.

Inbound works in the opposite way. You don't reach out to the customer; they reach out to you. And there are many inbound marketing techniques you can use to make sure you don't lose out when this happens.

The Outbound and Inbound Buying Process

To understand why inbound might work as well, or even better, than outbound marketing, just stop to think about your own buying process. How often are you swayed by outbound advertising or marketing that reaches out to you? When you see a billboard for Calvin Klein underwear, do you automatically rush to buy it? Or do you dismiss it right away, thinking it's not for you? The model might seem like an unreachable physical type, and the brand might seem too elite for a regular person.

But when it comes to inbound marketing, you usually hear about the product from a friend, either someone you know personally or a casual social media acquaintance. You might even hear about the product from a book you've read or a blogger you're following. There are many ways in which a person might just coincidentally hear about a certain product.

If you're skeptical about this, think about your own experiences. Don't you tend to follow up more on recommendations from friends, family, or business associates? When at least one person you know has had a good experience with a certain product or service, you think it's automatically more likely you will too. This is because these people are close to you; they're people you have something in common with.

The Honesty Inherent in the Inbound Process
Another reason inbound marketing works is because there's something more convincing about hearing it from real people who haven't been paid to promote anything. You know the model up there on the billboard is making money from being featured in the advertisement. But a friend or family member who recommended a product to you isn't being paid to do so.

This means the source from which you heard about the product or service is probably being much more honest. They'll tell you what they liked about the product, as well as what they didn't like. Even if they recommend it, they'll probably have a few words of caution. This is what tends to sway customers when it comes to inbound marketing—the honesty of the action.

Using Honesty to Your Advantage in Inbound Marketing

After someone recommends something, all the customer has to do is look it up on the internet and get more information about it. At this point, it's best for the company to keep their inbound marketing strategy as neutral sounding as possible. This doesn't mean they shouldn't be enthusiastic about their product. It's best, however, to avoid promotional/salesy content. What drew the customer to you in the first place was the honesty inherent in the recommendation. So, you need to continue this process by being honest with your customer too.

Most people can see through a sales pitch these days. Promotional writing is neither interesting nor persuasive anymore. If you really want to persuade your prospective customer, just try and give them as much information as possible. What are the different ways in which they can use your product? What are the different products featured in your product line? Testimonials from customers always have a ring of truth. Real-life stories and experiences are also interesting, as well as informative.

All this material can be added to your website, blog, or social media pages. And as you get more information, you can keep updating your online presence for better inbound marketing.

35

You've got to stop interrupting people who are on a Buyer's Journey to start selling. @BradFriedman

_____

_____

_____

36

I've always hated making cold calls. I much prefer closing deals. @BradFriedman

_____

_____

_____

37

Inbound marketing is about using available tools and awesome content to attract, understand, and WOW! customers. @BradFriedman

_____

_____

_____

38

Use it properly, and inbound marketing can make the sales cycle easier for salespeople and buyers too. @BradFriedman

_____

_____

_____

39

Inbound marketing does not end when a visitor turns into a lead. @BradFriedman

_____

_____

_____

40

Actually talk to your customers. Use language they use. Talk about the things they talk about. Never feed salad to a lion. @JayAcunzo

_____

_____

_____

41

Start with "Why?" and get your audience's attention. Ask them, "How may I help you?"
@BradFriedman

42

Content marketing is like a first date. If all
you do is talk about yourself, there won't be
a second date. @davidbeebe

_____

_____

_____

43

People don't buy what you do, they buy why you do it. @simonsinek

_____

_____

_____

44

Success is making those who believe in you look brilliant. @dharmesh

_____

_____

_____

45

People shop in a whole new way, so
marketers need to adapt or risk extinction.
@bhalligan

_____

_____

_____

46

Don't interrupt what your buyers want to
consume -- BE what they want to consume.
@mvolpe

_____

_____

_____

47

Own your words. Your words are the maps to your intentions. @chrisbrogan

_____

_____

_____

48

People trust people more than they trust institutions. @jchernov

_____

_____

_____

49

Tell a story. Make it true. Make it compelling.
And make it relevant. @randfish

_____

_____

_____

50

Common sense isn't optional. Don't do
stupid. @jillrowley

_____

_____

_____

51

How do you know your content is relevant? Increased social traffic, social engagement, and higher quality leads. @JasonMillerCA

_____

_____

_____

52

Invite people into your brand and lean into the possibilities. Build movements, not campaigns! @Ekaterina

_____

_____

_____

53

As with any relationship, the market favors those who give more value than they ask for. @LeslieBradshaw

_____

_____

_____

Section IV
LinkedIn

How Are You Using LinkedIn?

How you use LinkedIn depends on what you are trying to achieve and who you want to connect with. LinkedIn is where you want to grow your network of professional contacts. With more than 500 million members, LinkedIn is the social network to use to help you build your stable of professional contacts and qualified leads. If you want to network with serious decision makers, LinkedIn is the place to be. Here are few tips to help you generate business opportunities:

- At least once or twice a week, you must use LinkedIn to connect with current and former people you know. The goal is for people to have you in mind when an opportunity arises and your skill set is required.

- Every month, commit to joining a couple of LinkedIn Groups. The goal is to increase visibility while building trust and credibility. LinkedIn Groups are also a great way to grow your network. Joining is just the beginning, however. You must participate in the Group on a regular basis. Starting and participating in discussions gets your name in front of people and lets them know you are a thought leader.

- Each week, commit to sending a specific number of Inmails to people you aren't connected with.

Remember, your goal is to build your network with new connections, strengthen existing relationships, and position yourself as a trusted, credible thought leader so people want to provide you with leads and business opportunities.

Back to the LinkedIn Basics

Sometimes we get so caught up in everything going on around us, we make things more difficult than they need to be. This is easy to do with all the different social networks, each with its own set of rules and means by which we are to "socialize." Getting back to the LinkedIn basics will help. Keep these tips in mind, and you will be able to stay on track and make your LinkedIn experience more rewarding.

1. I can't emphasize enough how critical your profile is to your success on LinkedIn. Your profile is what people see first. You must put your best face forward. You only have one chance to make a first impression. Spend a lot of time perfecting your profile!

2. For people to find you on LinkedIn, you must employ search engine optimization techniques within your profile. Before doing anything, determine what keywords relevant to your work and industry will help you get found in search results. Once these words are determined, don't be shy about using them throughout your profile.

3. What separates LinkedIn from other social networks is its advanced search function. Use it often and assume others are

too. Use it to narrow in on what or who you are looking for. Craft your profile so you appear in results when others are searching too.

I emphasize the three tips above because LinkedIn allows participants to view profiles of other members within three degrees of separation from each other. Creating a robust profile and employing SEO techniques will increase the ability of people to see you and will help you build your network.

The same is true for LinkedIn Groups. Join them and then actively participate in them. This is a tremendous way to build credibility and grow your network. Be sure you join Groups relevant to your work and actively participate in each one you join. Add relevant information to the discussion—don't spam.

Connect with as many qualified people as you can. Connect with people who have many connections. You can send messages to direct connections whenever you wish. Do so to stay top of mind and to receive introductions to new connections.

Be sure people know where else they can find and connect with you. Let people know how to find you on Facebook, YouTube, and Twitter.

Stick with it. Like all social media, this is not a situation where, "if you build it, they will come." You need to devote a substantial amount of time to build a strong LinkedIn presence, build trust and credibility, and grow your network with qualified connections. Do this, and you will be rewarded for your efforts.

54

If Facebook is "like" a TGIF happy hour, LinkedIn is "like" a B2B networking event. @BradFriedman

_____

_____

_____

55

Before telling me you see no value in LinkedIn, Google yourself and tell me where your profile ranks in the search results. @BradFriedman

_____

_____

_____

56

Take 20 seconds to upload a professional-looking headshot to your LinkedIn profile, or don't expect me to connect with you.
@BradFriedman

57

Search bots start at the top of a page and work down. Fill your LinkedIn headline with keywords that tell us who you are.
@BradFriedman

58

Use your LinkedIn Summary to entice me to read the rest of your profile instead of just repeating what you said below. @BradFriedman

_____

_____

_____

59

Create the different sections of your LinkedIn profile in a Word document. Then use SPELLCHECK before you copy / paste! @BradFriedman

_____

_____

_____

60

LinkedIn is today's cold call, and you only have one chance to make a first impression. @BradFriedman

_____

_____

_____

61

Your job on LinkedIn is to attract prospects, not beg them. Present yourself in a way that attracts prospects to you. @BradFriedman

_____

_____

_____

62

Does your LinkedIn profile set the right tone to position you for the opportunities you're looking for? @BradFriedman

_____

_____

_____

63

Success on LinkedIn: "I'm a needle in a haystack. I need to be found by people who don't know they're looking for me." @BradFriedman

_____

_____

_____

64

There are over 500 million LinkedIn Users. A profile written without keyword research may never be discovered. @BradFriedman

_____

_____

_____

65

Your profile headshot need not be taken by a professional photographer so long as it's a headshot and LOOKS professional. @BradFriedman

_____

_____

_____

66

Active participation on LinkedIn is the best way to say, "Look at me!" without saying, "Look at me!" @cmcinc

_____

_____

_____

67

LinkedIn can connect you to information, insights, and people to be more effective. @reidhoffman

_____

_____

_____

68

LinkedIn is networking without the pressure. @melaniepinola

_____

_____

_____

69

Creating easy-to-read, relevant content showcasing the value of your service or product can lead to warmer leads. @zesanchezr

_____

_____

_____

70

LinkedIn and other social channels can greatly increase sales performance. @kenkrogue

_____

_____

_____

71

When you see that your prospect posted on LinkedIn 1 min. ago, you know they're online. Now's the time to reach out! @BradFriedman

---

72

The first thing you should do as a Social Seller is enhance your LinkedIn profile. Create a good impression before jumping in. @Kurtshaver

---

73

LinkedIn is a professional site. Your profile mustn't contain spelling or grammar errors & the photo should look professional. @BradFriedman

_____

_____

_____

74

Today, first impressions are digital. People learn about you on LinkedIn before shaking your hand. @BradFriedman

_____

_____

_____

75

Is your LinkedIn profile in its entirety
authentic, accurate, and real?
@BradFriedman

_____

_____

_____

76

What is it about your LinkedIn profile that helps you stand out from the hundreds of millions of LinkedIn users? @BradFriedman

_____

_____

_____

77

Does your LinkedIn profile address the needs of the prospects you are trying to attract? @BradFriedman

---

Section V
Social Media

Three Social Media Marketing Strategies to Try

Developing a social media marketing strategy is important. Just sticking with what you did last year is a mistake because, as you know, things are changing all the time and you need to keep up. You don't have to go as far as crumpling up your old plan and tossing it out, however. Take some time to analyze the data around what worked and didn't work last year, then try out at least one new social media marketing strategy. You may be pleasantly surprised with the results. Here are three good ideas to try.

#1. Establish Yourself as a Thought Leader

Rather than solely using your social media accounts to engage with your audience, use them to establish yourself as a thought leader in your industry. A thought leader is an individual whose opinions on a certain subject are given more authority than the opinions of others. Thought leaders are often the most successful in their fields, so it's something worth aspiring to.

To become a thought leader, you must deliver your own unique perspectives on news in your industry. Go deeper than summarizing it. Think about how the piece of news will impact different people. Develop strategies or plans to help them. There is a lot you can do; the key is to go beyond most professionals in your field and demonstrate your expertise.

#2. Try a New Social Media Platform

New social media sites pop up left and right. A few will become popular, whereas the rest either die off or fall somewhere in the middle. Typically, businesses that are the first to jump on a new social media platform that becomes popular benefit the most. Therefore, try one new social media platform this year to see how it goes. It will be exciting if it works out well for you. Be strategic, though. Join a platform where your target audience can be found.

An example of a younger social media platform to try is Periscope. Periscope launched in 2015 and is a live video streaming app that, as of January 2017, had 1.9 million daily active users. It's already popular and will likely continue the upward trend throughout the next few years.

#3. Re-purpose Content on All Platforms

An effective social media marketing strategy includes re-purposing your social media content on all the platforms you use. For example, you can upload a short clip from your YouTube channel to Twitter, Facebook, and LinkedIn. This allows you to get the most out of each piece of content. Think of the best way to present a social post on another platform. Remember, each social media site has different user demographics, psychographics, and culture. Reshape the post to match perfectly with the platform it will be posted on.

Consistently trying new social media marketing strategies is essential for growth and success. If you keep doing the same thing, you can't expect different results. You will lose touch with the changes occurring not only on social media sites but also on the internet. You will miss great opportunities to engage with your audience and grow your business. At the same time, you shouldn't try too many new things at once either. Just try at least one new strategy in your social media marketing plan this year.

78

Are you too old to change your thinking to believe there is a return on your investment in Likes, Shares, and Comments? @BradFriedman

_____

_____

_____

79

It takes 20 years to build a reputation and 5 minutes to ruin it. If you think about that, you'll do things differently. @WarrenBuffett

_____

_____

_____

80

Social Media is just another tool in your marketing toolbox. Integrate it into your overall plan to be successful. @BradFriedman

_____

_____

_____

81

People often share positive things in their life via social media, but how do you know what they're sharing is true?
@BradFriedman

_____

_____

_____

82

Some say, "Social Media is evil." I say these channels are tools. You decide how to use them. @BradFriedman

_____

_____

_____

83

Social Media doesn't kill people. People kill people. Don't hide behind your browser. Be human. Even online. @BradFriedman

_____

_____

_____

84

Social Media is a Give & Take. Don't lurk in the shadows, blasting out your messages. The word "Social" is there for a reason. @BradFriedman

_____

_____

_____

85

In the right hands, social media is a savior, an asset and a timesaver. Not an enemy, a liability, or a time-waster. @BradFriedman

_____

_____

_____

86

Business social media is the new cold call.
@gitomer

_____

_____

_____

87

Even an old guy like me has to admit social media is the new word of mouth marketing.
-- Financial Services Firm, Managing Partner

_____

_____

_____

88

Social media is now! Real-time, immediate value-add information will take your business to new levels faster than ever. @BradFriedman

_____

_____

_____

89

Put your name in a Google search. Your LinkedIn profile appears near the top of your results. Is it ready for primetime? @BradFriedman

_____

_____

_____

90

Social media is fluid. It's always changing. It's text, images, and video. It's real time. What are you doing to keep up? @BradFriedman

_____

_____

_____

91

Social media is on 24/7/365. To win, you MUST engage regularly and consistently and keep up. @BradFriedman

_____

_____

_____

92

Are you "all in" with social media? Do you still claim regulations keep you out? WAKE UP and look at your competition!
@BradFriedman

_____

_____

_____

93

Where do you think the Starbucks's plastic green stopper came from? Social engagement with customers is the answer.
@BradFriedman

_____

_____

_____

94

Does your business use Twitter for customer service like Comcast, Zappos, and other hugely successful companies? @BradFriedman

_____

_____

_____

95

It's not always about you. Successful companies recognize there is more to "social," and they spend time listening. @BradFriedman

---

96

Your customers have a voice. Listening, responding, engaging always results in revenue generation. @BradFriedman

---

97

How are you doing? What's your "Community Engagement" strategy? Are you Listening? Who do you engage with? @BradFriedman

_____

_____

_____

98

When was the last time you asked your customers what they consider valuable to know about you and your business? @BradFriedman

_____

_____

_____

99

Lagging behind the competition is one thing. Failing to meet customer's needs is different. What are you doing to keep up?
@BradFriedman

_____

_____

_____

100

Develop your social presence not to sell. Instead, build your community with people who want to buy. @BradFriedman

_____

_____

_____

101

My guess is your social presence is lacking because your foresight is being crippled by your insight. @BradFriedman

_____

_____

_____

102

Are you a social media believer or nonbeliever? Don't know? Check to see how far behind the competition you are. @BradFriedman

_____

_____

_____

103

Posting value-add content on your business pages about your product, service, or industry is guaranteed to attract prospects. @BradFriedman

_____

_____

_____

104

Your writing, your email newsletter, your reputation in your industry and community all affect your social media presence. @BradFriedman

---

105

Billions of dollars are being made by building social media communities. How big is your piece of the pie? @BradFriedman

106

Your social presence requires work, regular & consistent posts & engagement with followers. Anything less & you're invisible. @BradFriedman

_____

_____

_____

107

If you want to be relevant in the
Twitterverse, post something relevant.
No one cares what you ate for lunch.
@BradFriedman

108

Reposting your content any number of
times over the course of a year allows you to
literally get the most out of the content.
@BradFriedman

109

It's not just about consuming content but also sharing it, passing it on, and adding to it. @ariannahuff

_____

_____

_____

110

Buying Friends, Followers, and the like looks good on paper but becomes a terrible mistake. @BradFriedman

_____

_____

_____

111

If someone doesn't appreciate your online presence, make them appreciate your absence. @BradFriedman

_____

_____

_____

112

Be the reason someone looks down at their phone, reads value-add content, and walks into a pole. @BradFriedman

_____

_____

_____

113

If you are my friend but we're not connected via social media, are we really friends? @BradFriedman

_____

_____

_____

114

Never forget, online and off, you represent
the voice of your business 24 / 7 / 365.
@BradFriedman

_____

_____

_____

115

Be yourself, because an original is always worth more than a copy. --Unknown

_____

_____

_____

116

In a world where everyone acts like showing emotion makes you weak, businesses appreciate those who feel free to share. @BradFriedman

_____

_____

_____

117

I don't like to think before I tweet. I like to be just as surprised as everyone else about what comes out of my mouth.
@BradFriedman

_____

_____

_____

118

Sometimes deleting your reply before clicking "Post" is the best reply of all. @BradFriedman

_____

_____

_____

119

Having a terrible online presence is no better than not having one at all. The trick is recognizing "Terrible." @BradFriedman

_____

_____

_____

120

Don't treat people as bad as they act online.
Treat them as good as YOU are.
@BradFriedman

_____

_____

_____

121

Snapchat can make even the most talented realize how long 10 seconds actually is. @BradFriedman

_____

_____

_____

122

Yes! Snapchat is for your business. But only if you do it well. @BradFriedman

_____

_____

_____

123

If you're always the snapper and never the snapee, then maybe you're doing something wrong. Think about it. @BradFriedman

_____

_____

_____

124

Regardless of their popularity, if your business isn't image friendly, there's no need for Instagram or Pinterest. @BradFriedman

_____

_____

_____

125

Instagram Stories should be just that. A very short story with a beginning, middle, and end. @BradFriedman

---

126

Your business photo doesn't need to be taken by a professional photographer so long as it LOOKS professional. @BradFriedman

---

127

A picture is worth 1000 words. A GREAT
picture can be worth 1000 dollars.
@BradFriedman

_____

_____

_____

Section VI
Twitter

As I write this book, there appears to be some uncertainty about the future of Twitter. Will it survive on its own or get purchased by a media company? Will it shut down Periscope and go exclusively with Twitter Live? No one knows for sure.

What I do know is Twitter can be a valuable tool for your business to utilize. It's great for gathering breaking news in your industry and elsewhere, but it is best used for sending people somewhere with a link (your website, a blog post, or white paper). Here are ten ideas to help you use Twitter for your business:

1. Connect daily with followers in short, concise messages. Your followers will be thrilled to hear you are "just checking in" to see how they are doing. This tactic is great for building relationships, trust, and credibility.

2. Follow news and keep up with breaking news as it happens. This can be industry-specific news, political news, or regional news you're interested in. Twitter is the first place people post photos and video about breaking news.

3. Answer product or service-related questions, as well as customer service related issues. This tactic has many benefits. You're answering questions in a public forum, where others can also get this information, and you're showing the world

how you handle customer support issues and resolve problems quickly and efficiently.

4. Use hashtags to organize posts you're interested in, and keep up with specific groups of people and topics.

5. Use hashtags to perform competitive research.

6. Create and participate in social media events like Twitter Chats, where you demonstrate your knowledge and build trust, credibility, and thought leadership.

7. Retweet content you enjoy and content you think your followers will enjoy. This also helps you build trust and credibility, since you are sharing someone else's content and not just using Twitter to sell.

8. Remember, the more you connect with followers, the more likely they are to refer others to you.

9. If you're "feeling it," be sure to support causes you care about, so your followers get some insight into issues important to you.

10. Use Twitter to connect to other brands and thought leaders.

128

Twitter is great for sending people somewhere else! Get my attention with an image or video, then I'll click on your link. @BradFriedman

_____

_____

_____

129

Ever spent an hour doing competitive research on Twitter? Yes, I'm talking to you! @BradFriedman

_____

_____

_____

130

30 seconds after anything important happens anywhere in the world, you can read & see it on Twitter. Where's your new product? @BradFriedman

_____

_____

_____

131

Twitter reminds my mother of the saying,
"I heard it from a little birdie." I thought it
reminded her of her carrier pigeons.
@BradFriedman

132

It's hard to tweet! Henry Thoreau said, "Not that the story need be long, but it will take a long while to make it short."
@BradFriedman

133

Many question the value of Twitter. But with several hundred million users, there's sure to be some bucks in there. @BradFriedman

134

To be relevant on Twitter, post value-add content. Before you tweet, think, "Does this add value to my followers' day?"
@BradFriedman

_____

_____

_____

135

I don't do Twitter because I don't want to talk about myself more than I already have to. @kitharingtoncom

_____

_____

_____

136

The idea of Twitter started when I worked in dispatch, where taxis would broadcast where they were and what they were doing. @jack

_____

_____

_____

137

Twitter closes the six degrees of separation to one degree of separation. @garyvee

_____

_____

_____

138

On Twitter, our goal is to get people to follow us. In real life, that scares us and we call the cops. @BradFriedman

_____

_____

_____

139

Twitter is not a fad. It's a discussion about your product or service. And it's happening with or without you. @BradFriedman

_____

_____

_____

140

My father said, "If you take one second to think before you speak, you'll be in less trouble." Think before you tweet!
@BradFriedman

_____

_____

_____

About the Author

Brad Friedman, founder and president of The Friedman Group, LLC, is a Denver native, "Recovering Attorney," and author of *Brad Friedman on Digital Marketing—Doing Social Media Right, When You Don't Have the Time and Don't Want to Get in Trouble*.

Drawing on his lifetime of work with attorneys, CPAs, financial services providers, and business owners, Brad formed The Friedman Group to work with people to enhance their online presence, while helping them take advantage of the power of social media and inbound marketing.

Brad is one of the Top 100 Digital Marketing Influencers and one of the Top 100 Social Media Marketing Influencers in the World. In 2016 and 2017, his blog was named one of the Top 100 Social Media Blogs in the World.

Brad is available to speak or lead a workshop at your next conference. Visit https://friedmansocialmedia.com/services/guest-speaking/ for details and to get in touch with Brad.

AHAthat makes it easy to share, author, and promote content. There are over 40,000 quotes (AHAmessages™) by thought leaders from around the world that you can share in seconds for free.

For those who want to author their own book, we have time-tested proven processes that allow you to write your AHAbook™ of 140 digestible, bite-sized morsels in eight hours or less. Once your content is on AHAthat, you have a customized link that you can use to have your fans/advocates share your content and help grow your network.

➲ Start sharing: http://AHAthat.com

➲ Start authoring: http://AHAthat.com/Author

Please go directly to this book in AHAthat and share each AHAmessage socially at
http://aha.pub/DigitalMarketing

www.ingramcontent.com/pod-product-compliance
Lightning Source LLC
LaVergne TN
LVHW012200040326
832903LV00003B/29